Brainstorming:
It's Raining Ideas!

written by Terri Kelley
illustrated by Milena Radeva

ISBN-13:978-1481950879
ISBN-10:1481950878

I dedicate this book to my mother, Hyo Son West.
She was better known by the American name
my father gave her
when she first immigrated to America,
Sunshine.
All who knew her would agree that this name suited her
well. Although she suffered most of her adult life with
rheumatoid arthritis, she remained vigilant in her desire
to raise my brother and me in a happy
and safe environment as well as to take care of
our father as he went to work every day outside our
home. For this and
for too many other
reasons to list,
I respect and love
her immensely.
I miss her every day
and look forward to
the time when we
will be together again.

Today we write our story
or so my teacher said.
I've decided I will write
about my best friend, Fred.

Ms. Watkins gave us paper
and our pencils are all ready.
I'm writing about yesterday when
I went to the park with Freddy.

But wait, what's this? We can't start yet?
There's something we must do?
Brainstorming? What is that?
I haven't got a clue!

My teacher says, "It's like it's raining words, you write a list of things about the topic that you would like. You give your ideas wings!"

Fred Park

So here I go, I first write "Fred"
and to the list I add

"park" and "fun" and also "slide".
Ms. Watkins says, "Not bad…"

lide

Once I have a list of things,
Ms. Watkins sits by me.
"A good beginning," so she says.
"Can you think of more than three?"

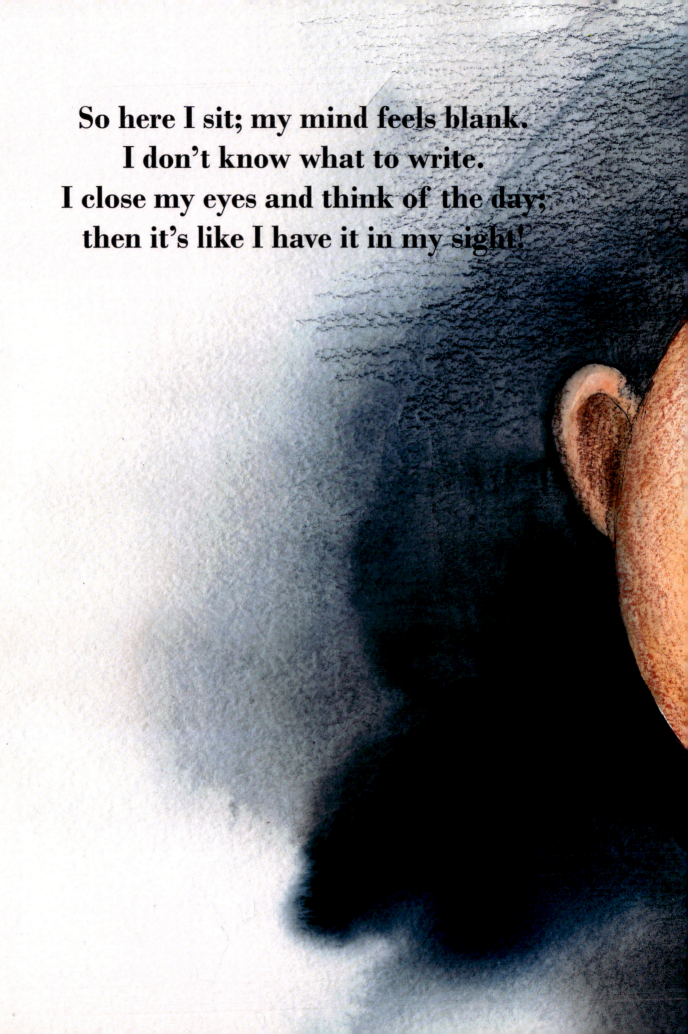

So here I sit; my mind feels blank.
I don't know what to write.
I close my eyes and think of the day;
then it's like I have it in my sight!

There was a dog that followed us.
We threw a stick for him.
When he couldn't find the stick,
he came back dragging a tree limb!

Words Words

And while I sat remembering
my mind did a cool new trick.
It started flashing different words
I could use about the dog and the stick.

Words

I opened my eyes and began to write
the words to describe the day:
"friendly dog", "fetching stick".
Once I began I had so much to say.

To the list I had begun
I added a few more words.
I included details about the day
like seeing a big black bird.

When I was done with my new list
I knew I was ready to begin.
From now on I will brainstorm first
to remember what has been.

te our story
her said.
will write
friend, Fred.

per
eady.
lay when
ddy.

Other Books in the Writing is a Process Series,
written by Terri Kelley:

Writing is a Process
Publishing: Finally it's Final!
Rough Drafts: Bumpy Writing is OK
Editing: It's Time for Corrections
Conferencing: Let's Talk it Over
Revising: It's Time to Make a Change
Presenting: It's Time to Share

Check out other books written by Terri Kelley as well.
Go to: www.terriLkelley.com for more information
or find her on Facebook at Terri Kelley Books.

About the Author

Terri Kelley, M.Ed, is the author of many children's picture books as well as of the chapter book series, "Gingerly". Her passion for writing and reading began when she was a very young girl. She was raised in Copperas Cove, Texas where she grew up in the country with horses and lots of freedom to explore her environment. It was a idyllic childhood.

As an adult, Terri has held a couple of different careers. Her previous one was as a teacher and reading specialist in Tomball, TX. It was there that she became aware of the kinds of books children enjoyed reading. She also noticed areas in need of good children's books.
You will find many of her books respond to these needs.

Terri is very happily married to her best friend, Michael. Together, they live in Eugene, OR with their black Labrador, Oliver. Terri and Michael enjoy traveling together, fishing, going to the movies, and, of course, reading great books. They have many good friends with whom they enjoy spending time as well.

If you would like to write to Terri, please visit her author's bookstore at **www.terrikelleybooks.com** or send an email to **terri@terrikelleybooks.com**.
She will make every effort to reply to your email as soon as she is able.
Thank you and happy reading!